D1479430

EXPLORE THE U.S.A.

NEW JERSEY

Megan Kopp

www.av2books.com

Go to www.av2books.com,
and enter this book's
unique code.

BOOK CODE

X150400

AV² by Weigl brings you media
enhanced books that support
active learning.

AV² provides enriched content that supplements and complements this book. Weigl's AV² books strive to create inspired learning and engage young minds in a total learning experience.

Your AV² Media Enhanced books come alive with...

Audio
Listen to sections of
the book read aloud.

Video
Watch informative
video clips.

Embedded Weblinks
Gain additional information
for research.

Try This!
Complete activities and
hands-on experiments.

Key Words
Study vocabulary, and
complete a matching
word activity.

Quizzes
Test your knowledge.

Slide Show
View images and
captions, and prepare
a presentation.

... and much, much more!

Published by AV² by Weigl
350 5th Avenue, 59th Floor
New York, NY 10118
Website: www.av2books.com   www.weigl.com

Library of Congress Cataloging-in-Publication Data

Kopp, Megan.
 New Jersey / Megan Kopp.
    p. cm. -- (Explore the U.S.A.)
 Includes bibliographical references and index.
 ISBN 978-1-61913-379-2 (hard cover : alk. paper)
 1. New Jersey--Juvenile literature. I. Title.
 F134.3.K67 2012
 974.9--dc23
                              2012015090

Printed in the United States of America in North Mankato, Minnesota
1 2 3 4 5 6 7 8 9 16 15 14 13 12

052012
WEP040512

Project Coordinator: Karen Durrie
Art Director: Terry Paulhus

Weigl acknowledges Getty Images as the primary image supplier for this title.

NEW JERSEY

Contents

3

4

This is New Jersey. It is the Garden State. Many fruits and vegetables are grown in New Jersey.

This is the shape of New Jersey. It is in the east part of the United States. New Jersey borders New York, Delaware, and Pennsylvania.

Where is New Jersey?

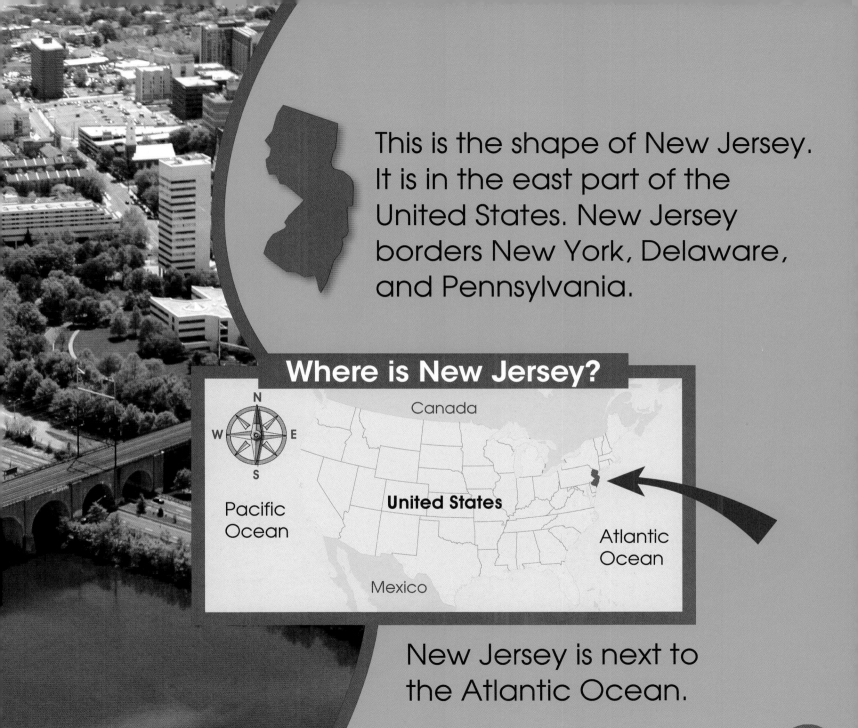

Canada

Pacific Ocean

United States

Atlantic Ocean

Mexico

New Jersey is next to the Atlantic Ocean.

American Indians lived in New Jersey more than 10,000 years ago. In the 1600s, three different countries all wanted to control the area.

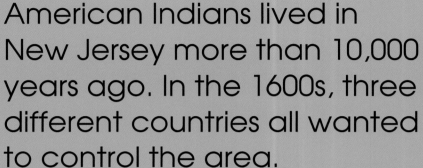

New Jersey became the third state in 1787.

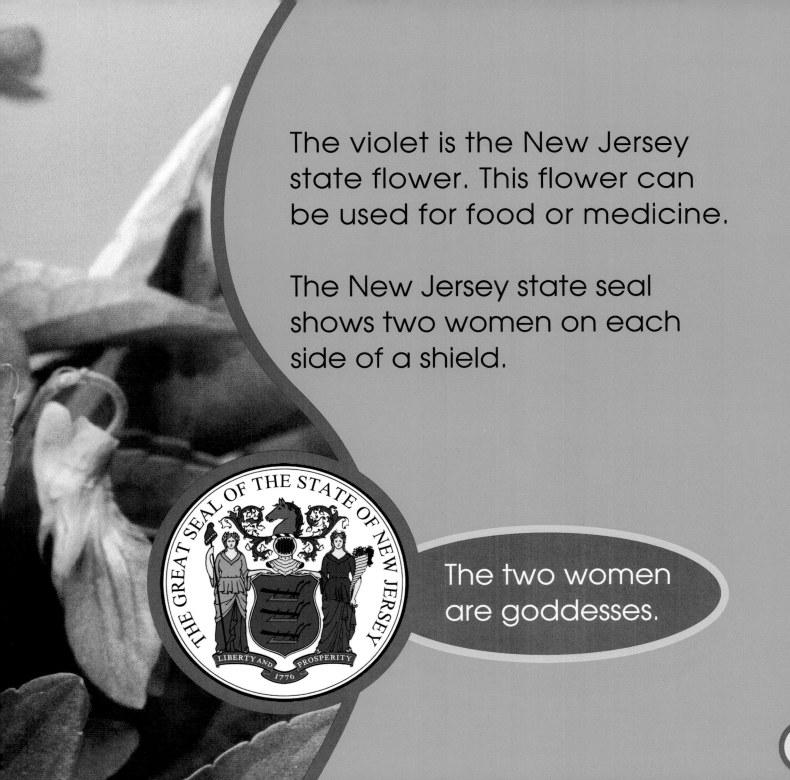

The violet is the New Jersey state flower. This flower can be used for food or medicine.

The New Jersey state seal shows two women on each side of a shield.

The two women are goddesses.

This is the state flag of New Jersey. The flag is a yellowish-brown color called buff.

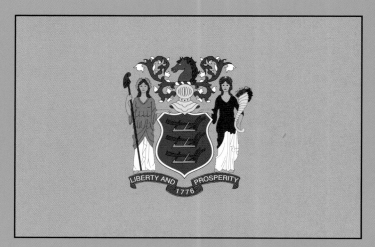

The state motto is on the flag.

The state animal of New Jersey is the horse. Horses are known for their speed and strength.

New Jersey is home to more than 42,500 horses.

Trenton is the capital city of New Jersey. It was named after a local judge named William Trent.

Trenton was once the capital city of the United States.

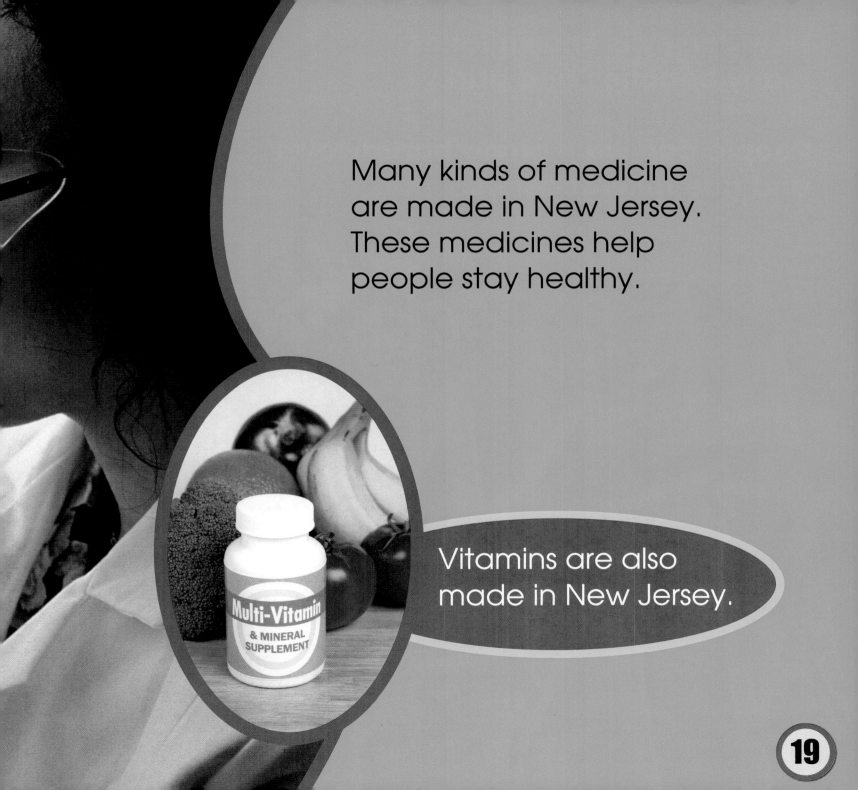

Many kinds of medicine are made in New Jersey. These medicines help people stay healthy.

Vitamins are also made in New Jersey.

New Jersey is known for its many beaches and parks.

People can walk along boardwalks and ride rollercoasters.

NEW JERSEY FACTS

These pages provide detailed information that expands on the interesting facts found in the book. These pages are intended to be used by adults as a learning support to help young readers round out their knowledge of each state in the *Explore the U.S.A.* series.

Pages 4–5

New Jersey is called the Garden State. Early settlers relied on the land for their living. New Jersey still has thousands of family-run farms. Today, the state has about 10,300 farms covering 790,000 acres (320,000 hectares). Cranberries are a popular crop, with about 3,500 acres (1,400 ha) of cranberry bogs in the state.

Pages 6–7

On December 18, 1787, New Jersey joined the United States as the third state. Except for the 50-mile (80-kilometer) northern border it shares with New York, New Jersey is surrounded by water. The Atlantic Ocean lies to the east. The Hudson River separates New Jersey from New York City. The Delaware River and Delaware Bay separate New Jersey from Pennsylvania.

Pages 8–9

American Indians settled in what is now New Jersey more than 10,000 year ago. In the mid-1600s, the Dutch, the British, and the Swedish struggled for control of the region. During the American Revolution, more than 100 battles were fought on New Jersey soil.

Pages 10–11

The common meadow violet became the official state flower in 1971. The state seal was presented to the New Jersey legislature in 1777. There are two goddesses pictured on the seal. On the left is Liberty. The liberty cap on her staff was worn as a symbol of rebellion during the American Revolution. Ceres, on the right, is the Roman goddess of grain.

Pages 12–13

The coat of arms from the state seal is in the center of the New Jersey flag. The knight's suit of armor with the helmet facing forward represents self-control. Below the helmet, a shield with three plows shows the importance of agriculture to the state's economy. The state motto, Liberty and Prosperity, is displayed on a banner underneath the shield.

Pages 14–15

The horse became New Jersey's state animal in 1977. A horse head is also found on the state seal. Horses were important to early farmers in the state, and people still raise horses in New Jersey today.

Pages 16–17

Originally called "Trent-towne," Trenton is named for New Jersey's first resident chief justice, William Trent. In 1784, Trenton was the capital of the United States for two months until a more permanent location was chosen. Trenton became the capital of New Jersey in 1790.

Pages 18–19

In the 1700s, New Jersey was known for glass blowing and iron forging. Today, the state is the leading producer of pharmaceuticals and chemicals. New Jersey has been nicknamed the "Nation's Medicine Chest." The state produces about one third of all the medicine approved by the U.S. Food and Drug Administration.

Pages 20–21

New Jersey has almost 1,800 miles (2,900 km) of shoreline. Beaches attract many visitors to the state. Atlantic City has 4 miles (6.4 km) of wooden boardwalk with entertainment, hotels, and amusement park rides.

KEY WORDS

Research has shown that as much as 65 percent of all written material published in English is made up of 300 words. These 300 words cannot be taught using pictures or learned by sounding them out. They must be recognized by sight. This book contains 51 common sight words to help young readers improve their reading fluency and comprehension. This book also teaches young readers several important content words, such as proper nouns. These words are paired with pictures to aid in learning and improve understanding.

Page	Sight Words First Appearance
4	and, are, in, is, it, many, state, the, this
7	next, of, part, to, where
8	all, American, different, Indians, lived, more, than, three, years
11	a, be, can, each, food, for, on, or, shows, side, two, used
15	animal, home, their
16	after, city, named, once, was
19	also, help, kinds, made, people, these
20	along, its

Page	Content Words First Appearance
4	fruits, garden, New Jersey, vegetables
7	Atlantic Ocean, Delaware, New York, Pennsylvania, shape, United States
8	area, countries
11	flower, goddesses, medicine, seal, shield, violet, women
12	color, flag, motto
15	horse, speed, strength
16	capital, judge, Trenton, William Trent, United States
19	vitamins
20	beaches, boardwalks, parks, rollercoasters

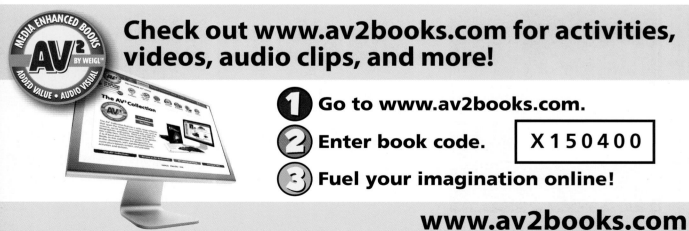